Little Pebble™

Transport

Trains

by Mari Schuh

Raintree is an imprint of Capstone Global Library Limited, a company incorporated in England and Wales having its registered office at 264 Banbury Road, Oxford, OX2 7DY – Registered company number: 6695582

www.raintree.co.uk
myorders@raintree.co.uk

Edited by Carrie Braulick Sheely
Designed by Lori Bye
Picture research by Wanda Winch
Production by Katy LaVigne
Originated by Capstone Global Library Limited
Printed and bound in India

ISBN 978 1 4747 4431 7 (hardback)
21 20 19 18 17
10 9 8 7 6 5 4 3 2 1

ISBN 978 1 4747 4437 9 (paperback)
22 21 20 19 18
10 9 8 7 6 5 4 3 2 1

British Library Cataloguing in Publication Data
A full catalogue record for this book is available from the British Library.

Acknowledgements
We would like to thank the following for permission to reproduce photographs: Alamy Stock Photo: Colin Underhill, 17, Jim West, 11; iStockphoto: BeyondImages, 15; Shutterstock: Albert Pego, 9, Bjorn Carlsson, 5, Dudarev Mikhail, 13, Frank Gaertner, 7, momente, 8, Sakarin Sawasdinaka, 21, Scanrail1, cover, Songquan Deng, 19, T. Sumaetho, zoom motion design

Every effort has been made to contact copyright holders of material reproduced in this book. Any omissions will be rectified in subsequent printings if notice is given to the publisher.

All the internet addresses (URLs) given in this book were valid at the time of going to press. However, due to the dynamic nature of the internet, some addresses may have changed, or sites may have changed or ceased to exist since publication. While the author and publisher regret any inconvenience this may cause readers, no responsibility for any such changes can be accepted by either the author or the publisher.

Contents

On the go

Choo choo!

The whistle blows.

The train is here.

All aboard!

People get into the train carriages.

The train leaves the station.

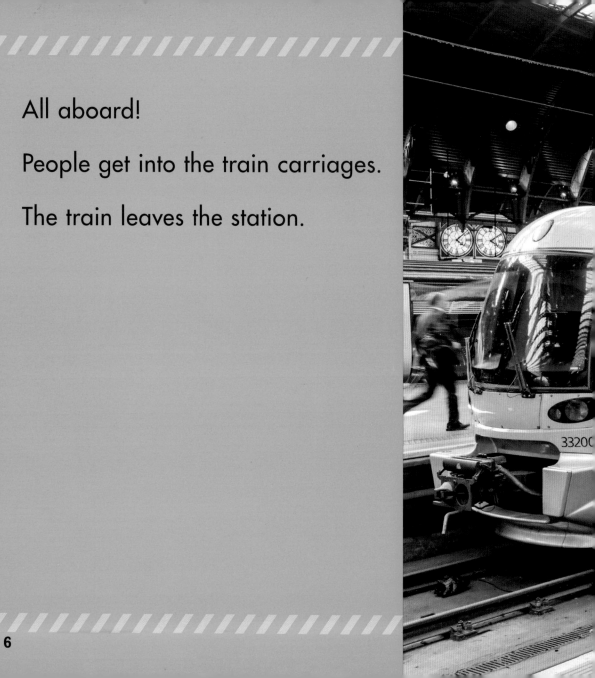

Parts

Look at the front of the train.

This is the locomotive. It pulls the train.

The engine is inside. It makes power.

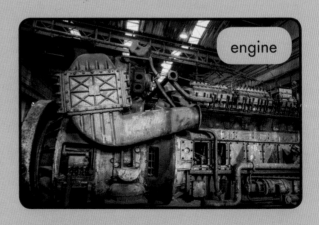

engine

locomotive

The cab is inside too.

The train driver sits in the cab.

He drives the train.

11

Look at the wheels.

They are made of steel.

They run on tracks.

Types

A freight train carries goods.

It can carry coal.

coal

Trains carry people to work.

They go into the city.

Some trains run under the ground.

They move under busy city streets.

Many people travel in them.

Way out →

Morden
Morden
11:22:53

A bullet train is fast and quiet.

It zooms by!

Are you ready for a train ride?

Glossary

cab area where the train driver sits

engine machine that makes the power needed to move something

locomotive railway car that holds the engine to move the train

station place where tickets for train journeys are sold and where people get on and off a train

steel strong type of metal

track set of steel rails that makes a path for trains

Find out more

Books

Big Machines Ride Rails! (Big Machines), Catherine Veitch (Raintree, 2015)

See Inside Trains (Usborne See Inside), Emily Bone (Usborne Publishing Ltd, 2013)

Trains (Usborne Beginners), Emily Bone (Usborne Publishing Ltd, 2011)

True or False? Transport, Dan Nunn (Raintree, 2014)

Websites

www.dkfindout.com/uk/transport/history-trains/
Learn the history of trains.

http://www.bbc.co.uk/education/clips/zpf34wx
Discover the importance of train travel in Victorian times.

Comprehension questions

1. How might people know that a train is coming?

2. What features make trains useful for carrying items?

3. In what ways do you think an underground system would be better than tracks that run above ground? In what ways could it be worse?

Index